Y2J

Pro Wrestler
Chris Jericho

by A. R. Schaefer

Reading Consultant:
Dr. Robert Miller
Professor of Special Education
Minnesota State University, Mankato

CAPSTONE
HIGH-INTEREST
BOOKS

an imprint of Capstone Press
Mankato, Minnesota

Capstone High-Interest Books are published by Capstone Press
151 Good Counsel Drive, P.O. Box 669, Mankato, Minnesota 56002
www.capstonepress.com

Library of Congress Cataloging-in-Publication Data
Schaefer, A. R. (Adam Richard), 1976–
    Y2J : pro wrestler Chris Jericho/by A. R. Schaefer.
    p. cm.—(Pro wrestlers)
    Includes bibliographical references (p. 45) and index.
    Contents: Undisputed champion—The early years—WCW—The WWF—Chris
Jericho today—Major matches—Y2J's hero—Rival in the ring.
    ISBN 0-7368-1313-6 (hardcover)
    1. Jericho, Chris—Juvenile literature. 2. Wrestlers—United States—Biography—
Juvenile literature. [1. Jericho, Chris. 2. Wrestlers.] I. Title: Y2J. II. Title. III. Series.
GV1196.J47 S32 2003
796.812'092—dc21   2001007721

Summary: Traces the personal life and career of professional wrestler Chris Jericho.

Editorial Credits
Angela Kaelberer, editor; Karen Risch, product planning editor; Timothy Halldin,
    series designer; Gene Bentdahl, book designer; Jo Miller, photo researcher

Photo Credits
AP/Wide World Photos, 41
Dr. Michael Lano, cover insets, 4, 7, 8, 12, 16, 19, 21, 22, 34, 38, 42
Geiger Kraig/CORBIS SYGMA, 36
Jason Szenes/CORBIS, 33
Rich Freeda/Getty Images, cover, 30
Scott Paymer/Getty Images, 29
Skye Dumoulin, 15, 25, 26

2 3 4 5 6 7 10 09 08 07 06 05

Capstone Press thanks Dr. Michael Lano, WReaLano@aol.com, for his assistance in
the preparation of this book.

Table of Contents

Chapter 1

Undisputed Champion

On December 9, 2001, professional wrestling fans gathered at the Sports Arena in San Diego, California. The fans were waiting to watch World Wrestling Federation (WWF) wrestlers compete at an event called Vengeance.

In March 2001, the WWF bought World Championship Wrestling (WCW). This wrestling company had been based in Atlanta, Georgia. Many WCW wrestlers joined the WWF. The WWF and WCW Championship titles were kept separate. But that fact would change at Vengeance. For the first time, one wrestler would

Chris Jericho hoped to become the Undisputed Champion of pro wrestling.

hold both the WWF and WCW World Championship titles. This wrestler would be the Undisputed Champion of pro wrestling.

First Match

Chris Irvine was ready to compete for the Undisputed Championship. He wrestles as Chris Jericho. First, Chris had to wrestle Dwayne Johnson. Johnson is known as The Rock. The Rock was the WCW World Champion. The winner of the match would wrestle WWF World Champion Steve Williams. Williams wrestles as "Stone Cold" Steve Austin.

Early in the match, Chris took The Rock down with one of his signature moves, the Lionsault. Chris did a backward somersault off the top rope. He landed on The Rock and went for the cover. But The Rock kicked out.

Later in the match, Chris charged into The Rock. The Rock slammed Chris to the mat with a spinebuster. The Rock then used the People's Elbow on Chris. He speared Chris with his elbow as he dropped to the mat. But Chris was able to get up.

Chris first wrestled The Rock for the WCW title.

Chris then used one of The Rock's signature moves. This move is the Rock Bottom. Chris stood next to The Rock. He wrapped his arm around The Rock's head and neck. Chris then picked up The Rock and slammed him to the mat. He covered The Rock's body as the referee counted to three. Chris had won the right to face Steve Austin for the Undisputed Championship.

After defeating The Rock, Chris faced Steve Austin for the Undisputed Championship.

Championship Match

Chris had wrestled The Rock for nearly 20 minutes. But he had no chance to rest before Austin ran into the ring.

Early in the match, Chris covered Austin for the pin. Austin kicked out. Austin then took Chris down with a Stone Cold Stunner. Austin stood in front of and slightly to the side of Chris. He wrapped his arm around Chris's head. Austin dropped to his knees as he slammed Chris to the mat.

Later in the match, Chris took Austin down with his other signature move, the Walls of Jericho. Chris pushed Austin down on the mat. He grabbed Austin's legs and put them underneath his arms. He then turned around to twist Austin's body. Austin crawled to the ropes and pulled himself up. Chris tried to punch Austin. Chris hit referee Earl Hebner instead and knocked him out of the ring. Chris then used Austin's move. He took Austin down with a Stone Cold Stunner.

Referee Nick Patrick ran into the ring to replace Hebner. Chris covered Austin as Patrick tried to make the count. But Richard Fliehr pulled Patrick out of the ring. Fliehr wrestles as Ric Flair. Austin took Chris down with a low blow. Chris got up and climbed to the top rope. He tried to take Austin down with a drop kick. Austin caught Chris and put him in the Walls of Jericho.

> ...After being here awhile, I thought that I had the qualities to be the Federation Champion...to have that happen is now the ultimate dream come true.
> –Chris Jericho, WWF.com, 12/10/01

Booker Huffman then jumped into the ring. Huffman wrestles as Booker T. He hit Austin with the WWF Championship belt. Hebner got back into the ring as Chris covered Austin. Hebner counted to three. Chris had become pro wrestling's first Undisputed Champion.

About Chris Jericho

Chris Jericho is one of today's most popular wrestlers. He is 6 feet (183 centimeters) tall and weighs 231 pounds (105 kilograms). Chris has many fans. He calls his fans "Jerichoholics."

Chris began wrestling in 1990. He wrestled for both Extreme Championship Wrestling (ECW) and WCW before joining the WWF in 1999. Chris has won many championships. In the WWF, he has won the World, Intercontinental, Tag Team, Hardcore, and European titles. He also has held the WCW World and Television Championships.

Major Matches

June 22, 1996—Chris defeats Pitbull 2 to win the ECW Television Championship.

June 28, 1997—Chris defeats Syxx to win the WCW Cruiserweight Championship.

August 10, 1998—Chris defeats Stevie Ray to win the WCW Television Championship.

December 12, 1999—Chris defeats Chyna for the WWF Intercontinental Championship.

April 2, 2000—Chris defeats Kurt Angle and Chris Benoit to win the WWF European Championship at WrestleMania 16.

May 21, 2001—Chris and Benoit defeat Triple H and Steve Austin to win the WWF Tag Team Championship.

October 21, 2001—Chris defeats The Rock to win the WCW World Championship.

December 9, 2001—Chris becomes the first Undisputed Champion of pro wrestling. He defeats The Rock to win the WCW World Championship and Steve Austin to win the WWF World Championship.

Chapter 2

The Early Years

Chris was born November 9, 1970, in New York City. His parents are Ted and Loretta Irvine. Ted was a professional hockey player. He played for the New York Rangers, St. Louis Blues, and Los Angeles Kings.

Chris grew up in Winnipeg, Manitoba, Canada. Chris liked to read and to act in school plays. He also was a good athlete. He played baseball, football, water polo, and hockey.

Chris became a professional wrestling fan as a child. He grew up watching the American Wrestling Alliance (AWA). The AWA held matches in Winnipeg once each month. Chris

Chris was born November 9, 1970, in New York City.

also watched Stampede Wrestling and the WWF on TV.

High School and College
Chris attended Westwood Collegiate High School in St. James, Manitoba. He graduated in 1988.

After graduation, Chris began classes at Red River College in Winnipeg. In college, Chris worked for wrestling promoter Bob Holliday. Chris helped set up and take down the ring at wrestling events. The job allowed him to talk to the wrestlers about their careers. In 1990, he graduated from Red River with a two-year degree in journalism.

A New Career
After college, Chris considered several careers. He could have used his journalism degree to write for a newspaper or magazine. He also thought about being a musician or an actor. He decided to become a pro wrestler instead. Chris believed he could use all of his talents in pro wrestling.

Chris believed he could use all of his talents in pro wrestling.

In June 1990, Chris attended the Hart Brothers School of Wrestling in Calgary, Alberta, Canada. Former wrestler Stu Hart trained many young wrestlers at this school in the basement of his home.

Chris graduated from Hart's school in September 1990. In October, he started wrestling for the Canadian National Wrestling

Chris wrestled in Mexico for two years.

Association (CNWA). Chris wrestled under his own name in matches in Alberta and Manitoba. He also formed a tag team with Lance Evers. Evers wrestles as Lance Storm. Their team was called Sudden Impact.

World Traveler

In October 1991, Chris went to Japan to wrestle for a company called Frontier Martial

Arts. Wrestling is popular in Japan. Wrestlers are paid well. But Chris did not like wrestling in Japan. He thought the company's style of wrestling was too different from North American wrestling. Chris returned to Canada.

In late 1992, Chris began wrestling in Mexico. In April 1993, Chris joined a large Mexican wrestling company called Empresa Mejicana de Lucha Libre (EMLL). He called himself Corazón de León. This name means "Lionheart" in Spanish.

Chris wrestled in Mexico for two years. He sometimes returned to Canada to wrestle for a company called Rocky Mountain Wrestling. On January 29, 1993, Chris defeated Biff Wellington for the Canadian Heavyweight Championship. Chris held the title only for about two weeks. But he was proud of his first championship.

In the EMLL, Chris teamed with wrestler Roberto Gutierrez. Gutierrez wrestles as El Dandy. On July 21, 1993, El Dandy and Chris defeated Texano and Silver King to win the World Wrestling Association Tag Team title.

> There are not a lot of wrestlers in this country who can go to a place like Japan... If guys think it is tough here, it is a million times tougher there.
> —Chris Jericho, *WOW Magazine*, 9/00

Chris continued to wrestle in Mexico and Canada during 1993 and early 1994. He won two more championships. In Mexico, he defeated Mano Negra to win the National Wrestling Alliance (NWA) Middleweight title. In Canada, he defeated Steve Rivers to win the Canadian Mid-Heavyweight title.

Success in Japan

In February 1994, Chris returned to Japan to wrestle for a company called WAR. He wrestled under the name Lion Do. This time, Chris had fun in Japan. Many times, Chris wrestled in the main event of the show. He became popular with the Japanese fans.

In Japan, Chris often wrestled Yoshihiro Asai. Asai wrestled as Ultimo Dragon. In November 1994, Ultimo Dragon defeated Chris for the NWA Middleweight title.

In Japan, Chris often wrestled Ultimo Dragon.

On June 4, 1995, Chris defeated Keiji Takayama to win the International Junior Heavyweight title. Takayama wrestles as Gedo.

Chris and Ultimo Dragon toured Japan for the next two months. They had a series of great matches. On July 28, the Dragon defeated Chris and took his title.

ECW

In February 1996, Chris joined Extreme Championship Wrestling (ECW). This wrestling company was based in Philadelphia, Pennsylvania. ECW was not as well known as the WWF or WCW. But the company had its own TV show and many fans.

Chris wanted a new wrestling name. He listened to a heavy metal band called Helloween. This band recorded a CD called *The Walls of Jericho*. Chris also liked the Bible story about the city of Jericho. Chris joined ECW as Chris Jericho.

On June 22, 1996, Chris wrestled Anthony Durante for the ECW Television title. Durante wrestled as Pitbull 2. Chris won the match and his first ECW title. Many people in the wrestling business were beginning to notice him.

Growing up, Chris sometimes became discouraged because most pro wrestlers were much bigger than he was.

Richard Blood showed Chris that a wrestler of his size could be successful. Blood wrestled as Ricky Steamboat. Steamboat is 5 feet, 10 inches (178 centimeters) tall. He weighed 235 pounds (107 kilograms) when he wrestled.

Steamboat was born in 1953. In 1976, he began wrestling with the NWA. In 1985, Steamboat joined the WWF. In 1987, he defeated Randy Savage for the WWF Intercontinental title at WrestleMania 3.

Steamboat later moved back and forth between WCW and the WWF. He won several WCW titles. In 1994, he retired after an injury.

Chapter 3

WCW

In the early 1990s, Chris met Canadian wrestler Chris Benoit in Japan. The two men later wrestled for ECW. Late in 1995, Benoit left ECW for WCW. He told WCW officials about his friend Chris Jericho. WCW offered Chris a contract.

Chris wrestled in his first WCW match on August 20, 1996. He defeated Jerry Lynn. At the time, Lynn wrestled as Mr. J. L.

On September 15, Chris wrestled Benoit at the Fall Brawl in Winston-Salem, North Carolina. Chris wrestled well, but Benoit won the match.

Chris Benoit helped Chris get a job with WCW.

On February 23, 1997, Chris wrestled for a WCW title. He faced Eddie Guerrero at SuperBrawl 7 in San Francisco, California. Guerrero was the U.S. Champion. Guerrero defeated Chris and kept the title.

First WCW Championship

Chris continued to work and train hard. WCW officials rewarded him with a chance at the Cruiserweight title. On June 28, 1997, Chris defeated Sean Waltman to win his first WCW title. At the time, Waltman wrestled as Syxx. Today, he wrestles as X-Pac.

In July, WCW officials set up a series of matches between Chris and Alex Wright. On July 28, Wright defeated Chris and took the title. Chris won the title back on August 12. He held the title for about one month before losing it to Eddie Guerrero on September 14.

That winter, Chris's WCW career changed. Wrestlers play a role during their matches. Some are heroes. These wrestlers are called "babyfaces" or "faces." Other wrestlers act mean to their opponents and the fans. These wrestlers are known as "heels." Chris had

Chris's signature move in WCW was the Lion Tamer. This move is much like the Walls of Jericho.

joined WCW as a babyface. But Chris now started screaming and throwing things in the ring. Fans soon turned against Chris. Within a few weeks, he became a heel.

On January 24, 1998, Chris regained the WCW Cruiserweight title. He defeated

In WCW, Chris often competed against Booker T.

Oscar Gonzales. Gonzales wrestles as
Rey Mysterio Jr.

Chris then started a feud with Dean Simon.
Simon wrestles as Dean Malenko. The two
wrestlers interfered in each other's matches.
They argued on TV. On May 17, 1998,
Malenko defeated Chris for the Cruiserweight
title. But Chris won it back on June 15.

Another Title

Chris then got an opportunity to wrestle for a different title. On August 10, 1998, Salvador Guerrero III challenged Lane Huffman for the WCW Television title. Guerrero wrestles as Chavo Guerrero. Huffman wrestles as Stevie Ray. Chris hit Guerrero before the match and knocked him out. Chris then wrestled Ray. Chris won the match and the title.

Chris held the Television Championship until November 30, 1998. On that night, he lost the title to Charles Ashenoff. Ashenoff wrestles as Konnan.

By early 1999, WCW officials seemed to have lost interest in Chris. He was still popular with the fans, but he did not get to wrestle in many good matches.

In April 1999, Chris wrestled Booker T for the Television Championship. Chris lost the match. He also injured his ankle.

Chris knew he needed to make a change in his career. He met with WWF officials about joining their company. In June 1999, the WWF signed Chris to a contract.

I always wanted to end up in this
company [the WWF], and now that I'm
here and had some measure of success,
it's like the dream coming full circle.
–Chris Jericho, *Canadian Press*, 9/19/01

Chris wrestled his last WCW match on July 21, 1999. It was a tag team match. Chris and Eddie Guerrero wrestled Rey Mysterio Jr. and Peter Gruner. Gruner wrestles as Billy Kidman. Before the match, Chris told the crowd he would leave WCW if he was pinned. Kidman pinned Chris. Chris was ready for a new start in the WWF.

Rey Mysterio Jr. was one of Chris's opponents during his final WCW match.

Chapter 4

The WWF

Chris wanted to make a big entrance during his first WWF appearance. One day, he was in the post office. He saw a millennium clock. This clock counted down each second until January 1, 2000. People called the year 2000 "Y2K." Chris got an idea.

During July 1999, the WWF's TV shows had a large electronic clock above the entrance. This clock counted down the seconds until August 9, 1999.

On August 9, the WWF was in Chicago, Illinois. Many fans held signs with Chris's name on them. As the show began, The Rock spoke to the fans from the middle of the ring.

Chris called himself "Y2J" when he joined the WWF.

31

The clock then ticked down to zero. Chris appeared at the entrance. Chris called himself "Y2J." He told the crowd that he was there to solve the WWF's problems. He said he would save the fans from boring wrestlers like The Rock.

First WWF Championship

Chris joined the WWF as a heel, but the fans cheered for him. On August 26, Chris wrestled his first WWF match. The match was against Brian James. James wrestles as Road Dogg. Chris powerbombed Road Dogg into a table. The referee then disqualified Chris.

On October 17, Joanie Laurer won the Intercontinental title from Jeff Jarrett. Laurer wrestled as Chyna. The next night, Chyna said she would wrestle anyone for the title. Chris came out on stage. He told Chyna that he would defeat her anytime. The next week, Chris asked Chyna to wrestle him. She refused.

Chris continued to argue with Chyna on the WWF's TV shows. On November 14, they met in the ring at Survivor Series in Detroit,

In 1999, Chyna was Chris's opponent during many WWF matches.

Michigan. Chyna defeated Chris and kept the Intercontinental title.

Chris and Chyna continued to argue for the next few weeks. On December 12, Chris again challenged Chyna for the Intercontinental title. Chris used the Walls of Jericho to defeat Chyna and win his first WWF title.

Rival in the Ring: Chris Benoit

Chris Jericho and Chris Benoit have much in common. Both are from Canada. They are about the same size. Both trained with Stu Hart. Both wrestled in Germany, Japan, and Mexico. Like Chris, Benoit wrestled in ECW and WCW before joining the WWF.

Benoit is 5 feet, 10 inches (178 centimeters) tall and weighs 220 pounds (100 kilograms). He began wrestling in Canada in 1986. Benoit has won many titles during his long career. These titles include the WCW World Championship, three WCW Tag Team Championships, and three WWF Intercontinental Championships. His signature move is the Crippler Crossface.

Chris and Benoit have wrestled against each other and as a team. They have wrestled three times for the WWF Intercontinental Championship. Chris won two of these matches. On May 21, 2001, Chris and Benoit defeated Steve Austin and Triple H for the WWF Tag Team Championship.

On December 30, Chyna challenged Chris for the title. At the end of the match, both wrestlers lay in the middle of the ring. One referee said Chyna was the winner. The other referee gave the match to Chris.

The referees could not reach a decision. The WWF gave the title to both wrestlers. Both wrestlers would lose the title if either lost a match. For a few weeks, Chyna and Chris worked together to successfully defend the title. But on February 27, 2000, Chris lost the title to Kurt Angle.

Another Title

On April 2, Chris won the European Championship at WrestleMania 16. He defeated Chris Benoit and Kurt Angle. Chris lost the title the next night to Eddie Guerrero. Only two weeks later, Chris got a chance to win a more important championship. He challenged Paul Levesque for the WWF World Championship. Levesque wrestles as Triple H.

On April 17, Chris met Triple H in the ring in State College, Pennsylvania. John Layfield

Chris had a chance to defeat Triple H for the WWF Championship in 2000.

and Ron Simmons were at ringside to help Chris. Layfield wrestles as Bradshaw. Simmons is Farooq. Shane McMahon was there to help Triple H. McMahon is the son of WWF owner Vince McMahon.

During the match, Triple H ran into referee Mike Chioda and knocked him down. Chris then hit Triple H with the World Championship belt. Chris covered Triple H, but Chioda could not get up to make the count.

Referee Earl Hebner then ran into the ring. Hebner counted to two, but Triple H kicked out. Chris took down Triple H with a spinning heel kick. Chris climbed to the top rope and landed a Lionsault on top of Triple H. Hebner quickly counted to three. Chris was the World Champion. He grabbed the belt and walked to the locker room.

In the ring, Triple H and Shane McMahon argued with Hebner. Triple H and McMahon said Hebner had counted too fast. Triple H and McMahon convinced Hebner to change his decision. Chris had to give back the belt. He had been the World Champion only 18 minutes. But Chris knew he had wrestled well. He would get another chance at the title.

Chapter 5

Chris Jericho Today

The year 2001 began well for Chris. On January 21, he defeated Chris Benoit to win his fourth Intercontinental title. In May, he teamed with Benoit to win the WWF Tag Team Championship. One week later, Chris defeated Paul Wight for the WWF Hardcore Championship. Wight wrestles as the Big Show.

Chris continued to win during the rest of the year. On October 21, Chris defeated The Rock for the WCW World Championship. The next night, Chris teamed with The Rock to win

Chris wrestled well during 2001.

another Tag Team title. They defeated Mark Lomonica and Devon Hughes. Lomonica and Hughes wrestled as the Dudley Boyz. In December, Chris became pro wrestling's first Undisputed Champion.

Chris held the Undisputed title until March 17, 2002. He lost the title to Triple H at WrestleMania 18 in Toronto, Ontario, Canada.

Outside the Ring

Chris enjoys heavy metal music. He first played in a heavy metal band in high school. Today, he is the lead singer of a heavy metal band called Fozzy. Chris calls himself Moongoose McQueen when he plays with Fozzy. He has recorded two CDs with his band.

Chris also likes to work with computers. He runs his own Internet site. This site includes articles and pictures about Chris.

Chris married Jessica Lockhart on July 30, 2000, in Winnipeg. They live near Tampa, Florida. Chris and Jessica have a dog named Blaze. They also have two ferrets named Cosmo and Saucy Jack.

Chris often helps charities. He especially likes to work with groups that help children.

Chris sometimes reads to children at libraries.

He has read to children at schools and
libraries. Chris also takes part in the New
York Rangers' SuperSkate. Actors, athletes,
and other celebrities play in this hockey game
at Madison Square Garden in New York City.
The money raised from ticket sales goes
to charities such as Rangers Cheering
for Children.

Career Highlights

1970—Chris is born November 9 in New York City.

1990—Chris graduates from Red River College and the Hart Brothers School of Wrestling.

1993—Chris wins his first professional title, the Rocky Mountain Wrestling Canadian Heavyweight Championship.

1996—Chris joins ECW in February as Chris Jericho and begins wrestling for WCW in August.

1997—Chris twice becomes the WCW Cruiserweight Champion.

1998—Chris wins the WCW Television Championship.

1999—Chris joins the WWF. Later that year, he wins the Intercontinental Championship.

2000—Chris defeats Triple H for the WWF World Championship; the referee later reverses the decision.

2001—Chris wins the WCW World Championship, the WWF Intercontinental Championship, and the WWF Hardcore Championship; he wins the WWF Tag Team Championship twice; in December, he becomes the first Undisputed Champion of pro wrestling.

Words to Know

contract (KON-trakt)—a legal agreement between a wrestler and a wrestling company

disqualify (diss-KWOL-uh-fye)—to prevent someone from taking part in or winning an activity; athletes can be disqualified for breaking the rules of their sport.

feud (FYOOD)—a long-running quarrel between two people or groups of people; wrestlers often have feuds.

journalism (JUR-nuhl-iz-uhm)—the work of gathering and reporting news for newspapers, magazines, and TV

millennium (muh-LEN-ee-uhm)—a period of 1,000 years

referee (ref-uh-REE)—a person who makes sure athletes follow the rules of a sport

signature move (SIG-nuh-chur MOOV)—the move for which a wrestler is best known; this move also is called a finishing move.

To Learn More

Alexander, Kyle. *Pro Wrestling's Most Punishing Finishing Moves.* Pro Wrestling Legends. Philadelphia: Chelsea House, 2001.

Burgan, Michael. *The Rock: Pro Wrestler Rocky Maivia.* Pro Wrestlers. Mankato, Minn.: Capstone High-Interest Books, 2002.

Hunter, Matt. *Superstars of Men's Pro Wrestling.* Male Sports Stars. Philadelphia: Chelsea House, 1998.

Kaelberer, Angie Peterson. *Triple H: Pro Wrestler Hunter Hearst Helmsley.* Pro Wrestlers. Mankato, Minn.: Capstone High-Interest Books, 2003.

Useful Addresses

Professional Wrestling Hall of Fame
P.O. Box 434
Latham, NY 12110

World Wrestling Entertainment, Inc.
1241 East Main Street
Stamford, CT 06902

Internet Sites

FactHound offers a safe, fun way to find Internet sites related to this book.

Go to *www.facthound.com*

He'll fetch the best sites for you!

Index